INDUSTRIAL AGE
MEDICINE

Rebecca Vickers

Raintree

Chicago, Illinois

EXPRESS
EDITION

www.capstonepub.com
Visit our website to find out more information about Heinemann-Raintree books.

To order:
☎ Phone 888-454-2279
💻 Visit www.capstonepub.com to browse our catalog and order online.

© 2013 Raintree
an imprint of Capstone Global Library, LLC
Chicago, Illinois

Edited by Andrew Farrow, Adam Miller, and Vaarunika Dharmapala
Designed by Philippa Jenkins
Picture research by Ruth Blair
Originated by Capstone Global Library Ltd
Printed and bound in China by Leo Paper Products Ltd

16 15 14 13 12
10 9 8 7 6 5 4 3 2 1

Library of Congress Cataloging-in-Publication Data
Vickers, Rebecca.
 Industrial age medicine / Rebecca Vickers.
   p. cm. — (Medicine through the ages)
 Includes bibliographical references and index.
 ISBN 978-1-4109-4663-8 (hb (freestyle express)) — ISBN 978-1-4109-4669-0 (pb (freestyle express)) 1. Medicine — History — 19th century. 2. Medicine — History — 18th century. 3. Industrial revolution. I. Title.
  R149.V53 2013b
  610 — dc23   2012001385

Acknowledgments
We would like to thank the following for permission to reproduce photographs: Alamy pp. 6 (© North Wind Picture Archives), 12, 24, 29 (© The Protected Art Archive), 32 (© Paris Pierce), 33 (© Vario Images GmbH & Co. KG), 39 (© Photo Researchers); Corbis pp. 10 (© The Gallery Collection), 23 (© Bettmann); Courtesy of NLM p. 28; Getty Images pp. 18, 26, 27, 35 (Hulton Archive), 21 (Buyenlarge), 22 (MPI), 30 (SSPL), 36 (Museum of the City of New York); Mary Evans Picture Library p. 14; Science Photo Library pp. 19 (Jim Varney), 20, 38 (National Library of Medicine), Wellcome Library, London pp. 4, 5, 8, 9, 11, 16, 19, 25, 31, 34, 37, 41.

Cover photograph of a painting of Florence Nightingale attending a patient at Scutari Barracks, Turkey, reproduced with permission of Alamy (© Mary Evans Picture Library).

Every effort has been made to contact copyright holders of any material reproduced in this book. Any omissions will be rectified in subsequent printings if notice is given to the publisher.

Disclaimer
All the Internet addresses (URLs) given in this book were valid at the time of going to press. However, due to the dynamic nature of the Internet, some addresses may have changed, or sites may have changed or ceased to exist since publication. While the author and publisher regret any inconvenience this may cause readers, no responsibility for any such changes can be accepted by either the author or the publisher.

Contents

Some words are shown in bold, **like this**. You can find out what they mean by looking in the glossary. You can also look out for them in the "Word Station" box at the bottom of each page.

Medicine on the Move

The ways people treat and prevent illness are known as **medicine**. In the mid-1700s, medicine began to quickly change and develop.

ET PLURIMA MORTIS IMAGO

This artwork shows that doctors were once viewed in a bad way. They were seen as overpaid, lazy, and dishonest. This view began to change in the mid-1700s, as doctors became better trained.

Becoming a doctor

The first **medical** school (college for studying medicine) in North America was started in 1765. Thanks to schools like this, people started to get better training to become doctors. But there were no set rules to become a doctor.

WORD STATION
medicine science of treating and preventing illness

Sticking to what they knew

Most doctors attended **dissecting** rooms as part of their training. Dissecting is cutting up a dead body to study it. This led to a good understanding of the parts inside the human body.

But in the mid-1700s, doctors' tools were very basic. And the way they **diagnosed** patients (identified what was wrong with them) was not usually based on science. Doctors did not understand the causes of many illnesses. This was all about to change.

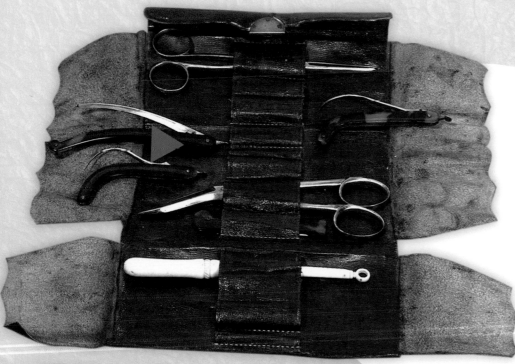

In the mid-1700s, most doctors could fit the tools available to them into a leather carrier like this.

Rapid changes

During the mid-1700s, something called the **Industrial Revolution** began. This was a period when machines changed daily life. **Factories**, which are large buildings with machines, made things to sell.

People moved from the country to the cities to work in new jobs, such as jobs in factories. The cities became crowded and dirty. These conditions led to the spread of many illnesses.

The Industrial Revolution led to crowded cities. Factories dirtied the air.

WORD STATION
factory large building with machines used to make things

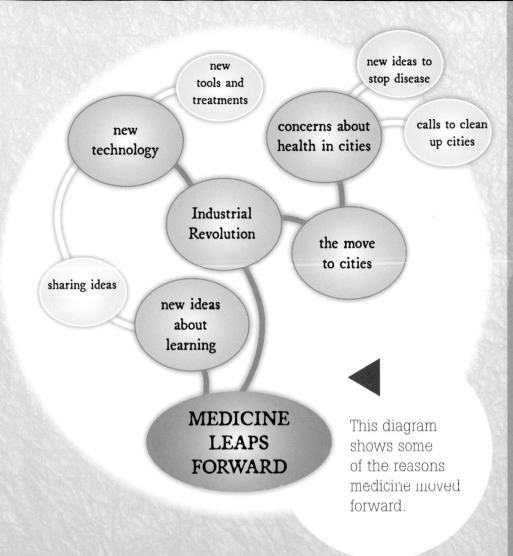

This diagram shows some of the reasons medicine moved forward.

Science and technology

The Industrial Revolution created a lot of new **technology** (machines and tools). This was often useful for **medicine**. For example, better technology led to improvements in glass-making. This made it possible to build better **microscopes**. Microscopes are tools used to look at very small objects.

New ideas about learning

During this period, doctors began to write down their discoveries. Doctors also tried to learn from and use other people's scientific discoveries. This allowed new ideas to spread.

Beginning to Understand Diseases

Starting in the mid-1700s, people began to better understand what causes **disease**. A disease is a health problem that prevents the body from working properly.

This is a microscope from the mid-1700s.

WORD STATION
disease health problem that prevents the body from working properly

Seeing the causes of disease

Improved **microscopes** meant that scientists could now see much smaller things. Some began to think that very small living things might have something to do with disease.

John Pringle researched **epidemics** in prisons, hospitals, and army camps. Epidemics are the quick spread of disease through an area or group of people. He noticed that when large numbers of people lived close together, disease spread quickly.

Pringle wondered if tiny living things could be connected to epidemics. He studied these living things with his microscope. (For more on his discoveries, see page 13.)

JOHN PRINGLE
(1707-1782)

John Pringle was a Scottish doctor. He worked to stop the huge numbers of deaths that happened whenever large groups of people lived close together.

Inoculation

The most feared of all major **diseases** at the time was **smallpox**. This disease killed many people. Those who did not die were often left blind. They also had terrible scars on their faces from the smallpox blisters.

Some people tried to protect themselves with a risky treatment called **inoculation**. This involved being exposed to **pus** (a thick yellowish substance) from the sores of someone with a mild case of smallpox. This would hopefully prevent the person from catching a more serious form of the disease. But there was always the chance that the disease could turn into a deadly form of smallpox.

MARY WORTLEY MONTAGU
(1689–1762)

Mary Montagu was an Englishwoman whose husband worked in the country of Turkey. While she was in Turkey, she witnessed smallpox inoculations. After her return, she introduced the method to England. Soon people could pay for inoculations. Later, Jenner's vaccinations replaced inoculations.

This cartoon from the early 1800s shows Jenner vaccinating patients. They are growing cow heads. This joke refers to Jenner's experiments with cowpox.

Edward Jenner's cowpox experiments

English doctor Edward Jenner noticed something. People who caught cowpox (a less serious form of smallpox) never got smallpox.

In 1796 he collected pus from a cowpox sore. He put it in a cut on the arm of an eight-year-old boy named James Phipps. James became a little sick, but he got better. Then Jenner gave James smallpox in the same way. Nothing happened! James's treatment with cowpox protected him from catching smallpox. This process became known as **vaccination**. Smallpox vaccinations quickly spread around the world.

WORD STATION
vaccination introducing a substance into the body so the person does not catch a disease

Cleaning Up Medicine

Edward Jenner gave the world of **medicine** a tool in the fight against **smallpox**. At the same time, other doctors were finding more ways to stop **diseases** from spreading.

These soldiers in a hospital tent from the Civil War (see pages 32 and 33) are wrapping wounds. Tents like this were dirty and dangerous. ▶

WORD STATION
microorganism very tiny living thing

Jail fever travels to the courts

In the mid-1700s, John Pringle (see page 9) and others noticed that diseases spread very quickly in crowded places. But they did not know why. Pringle noticed that an illness known as jail fever was causing **epidemics** in jails. The disease was also traveling with prisoners when they went to **court**, where judges decided on their punishments.

Destroying microorganisms

Pringle introduced a set of steps that included washing prisoners before they went to court. These steps worked. They stopped the spread of disease.

But people were slow to believe these ideas. This was because they did not know about **microorganisms**, or tiny living things. Microorganisms that can cause disease are called **germs**. If they are not washed away, they can move from one person to another, spreading disease.

(see page 9)

Average age at death in 1800	
United Kingdom	40
United States	39
Germany	38
Australia	35
France	32
India	25

This table shows how many years the average person could expect to live in these countries in 1800. This was often because doctors did not know how to prevent the spread of disease.

Germs: Small, but deadly

Many doctors and other scientists had seen tiny living things through **microscopes** or in drawings. But few people believed that living things were spreading **diseases**.

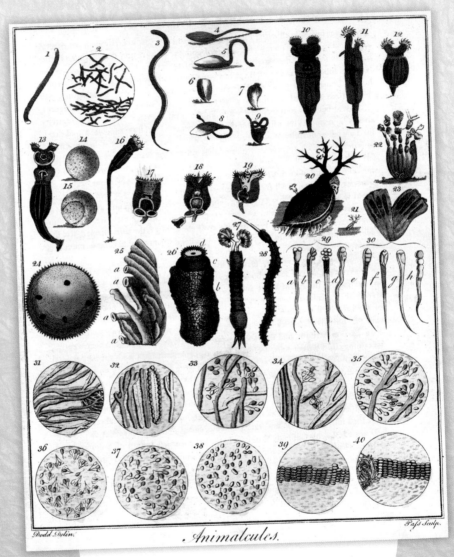

Animalcules.

These are some of the tiny living things described by scientists in the late 1700s.

WORD STATION
midwife specially trained nurse who helps women with childbirth

Ignaz Semmelweis

In 1844 Ignaz Semmelweis began working at a hospital in Vienna, in the country of Austria. Doctors from the hospital worked in one area for childbirth. **Midwives** worked in another. Midwives are nurses trained to help with childbirth. Semmelweis soon noticed that many more women were dying after childbirth in the doctors' area.

But why? The midwives only delivered babies. But the doctors also performed **autopsies** (examinations of dead bodies). They did not wash their hands or change their clothing between duties. The **germs** on them from dead patients caused **infections** in new patients. Infections are when tiny living things, like germs, enter a person's body and make the person sick.

Semmelweis got the doctors to wash their hands in an **antiseptic** before touching live patients. An antiseptic is a substance that kills germs. As a result, fewer people died. But most people at the time did not believe Semmelweis's ideas. He lost his job in 1849.

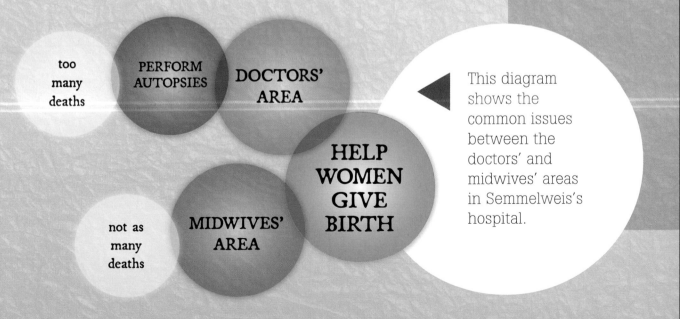

too many deaths

PERFORM AUTOPSIES

DOCTORS' AREA

not as many deaths

MIDWIVES' AREA

HELP WOMEN GIVE BIRTH

This diagram shows the common issues between the doctors' and midwives' areas in Semmelweis's hospital.

Understanding Germs

By the 1800s, many scientists had used **microscopes** to see things like **germs** up close. But most doctors and scientists still did not believe that germs caused **diseases**. Instead, they thought the germs were *created by* diseases. Then, a French scientist named Louis Pasteur proved them wrong.

This 1885 drawing shows Louis Pasteur using a microscope.

Proving the link

When Pasteur looked at sour alcohol under a microscope, he could see tiny living things. He suspected that germs were getting into the open containers of alcohol through the air. They **contaminated** it, or made it unclean.

To test his idea, Pasteur put water into a special container. It had a thin top part shaped like a swan's neck. He then heated the water to boiling. The boiling killed off any germs in the water. The rising warm air left the neck of the container, taking any germs with it.

Then, he broke the neck of the container. This left the clean water open to the air. It once again became contaminated with germs. This proved something. The germs themselves were able to contaminate something.

Matching germs to diseases

After this experiment, Pasteur went on to explore other ideas:

- He developed **pasteurization**. This involves heating substances like milk at specific temperatures to destroy germs. This keeps milk safe and fresh.

- He convinced many doctors that they should **sterilize** their equipment and tools. This means they should clean them to remove any harmful living things. This killed many of the germs that would have been spread from patient to patient.

Seeking the germs

Pasteur said the next step was to figure out which **germ** caused which **disease**. Only then could treatments be developed. In 1872 the German doctor Robert Koch did just that. He started to identify the germs that caused major diseases. The work of Koch and others made it possible to create new treatments.

A NEW SCIENCE

Robert Koch created important new ways to examine very small living things. These advances made it easier for scientists to study and group different kinds of tiny living things.

Robert Koch started his career as an army doctor.

Joseph Lister

Joseph Lister was a British **surgeon** (person who performs **surgery**). In the mid-1860s, he read about Pasteur's work. He realized that germs must also cause the **infections** that killed so many patients after surgery.

WORD STATION
surgeon person who performs surgery

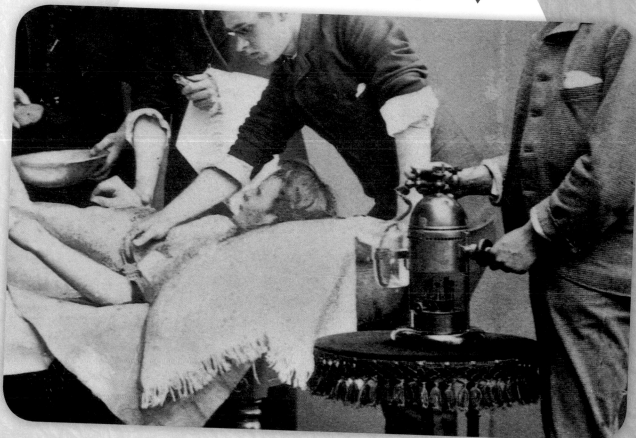

Joseph Lister used carbolic acid in operating rooms like this one. It was sprayed from the pump on the right.

Lister knew he would have to find some way to kill germs. He started to experiment with a substance called **carbolic acid**. Soaking bandages in carbolic acid meant that wounds were protected from infection during surgery. When all other parts of operating rooms were also sprayed with carbolic acid, far fewer patients died.

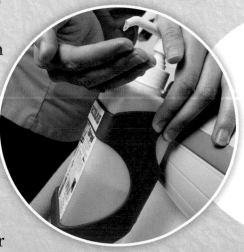

Today, **antiseptics** (see page 15) are still used to keep germs out of hospitals.

Hospitals

In the early 1800s, hospitals were mostly for sick poor people. Other sick people were usually treated at home. These hospitals were dirty and crowded. They did not offer many helpful treatments. But during the next 100 years, hospitals changed greatly.

What changed?

There were three main developments during the 1800s that changed hospitals:

- *Better training of doctors and nurses:* During the 1800s, teaching hospitals became common. In 1847 the American **Medical** Association was formed. This and similar groups set rules for doctors. Nursing schools also became common in the late 1800s.

This illustration is from 1807. People at the time often thought that nurses were not capable of helping patients.

WORD STATION
antiseptic substance that kills tiny, harmful living things

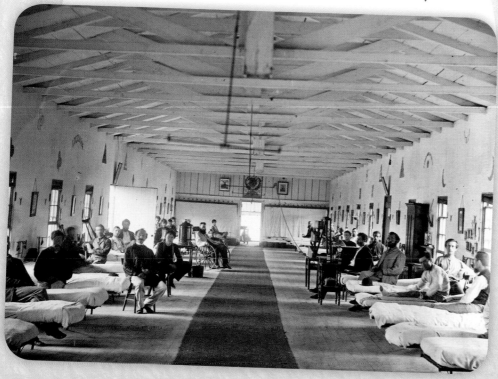

This photo of a military hospital in Washington, D.C., was taken in 1865. By this time, hospitals were becoming safer and more effective.

- *Technology developed*: Scientists used new **technology** to test and study **microorganisms** (tiny living things). This helped them deal with **disease**. New machines meant that hospitals could offer special services not available elsewhere.

- *Science changed*: As we have seen, scientists increasingly saw the importance of keeping clean. From the late 1860s, **antiseptics** were introduced to fight **germs**. This meant fewer people died from catching diseases and **infections** in the hospital. The development of pain control substances, called **anesthetics**, also made a difference (see pages 22 and 23). This meant that **surgery** could take longer. This led to more successful surgeries.

Preventing pain

In hospitals the pain of **surgery** could be unbearable to patients. So people wanted to find a way to stop the pain. In October 1846, a U.S. dentist named William Morton tried a substance called **ether**. The patient breathed in ether while a **surgeon** removed a growth from the patient's neck. This operation was a painless success.

Ether is being used on this patient during an operation in 1846.

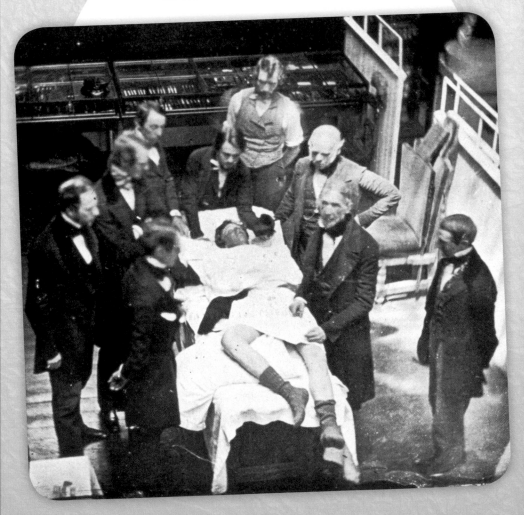

WORD STATION
ether strong substance that was breathed in to relieve pain

 The United Kingdom's Queen Victoria (seated) used chloroform to relieve pain during childbirth. Many people wanted to use chloroform for pain relief after she said that it worked well.

Chloroform

In 1847 Scottish doctor James Young Simpson wanted to find something other than ether. He worked with a substance called **chloroform** instead. It was stronger and faster-acting than ether. It was also easier to give to patients.

Chloroform became the most common **anesthetic** used until 1900. Ether then became more popular, after it was shown that chloroform caused serious health problems.

WHAT WAS WRONG WITH ETHER?

James Simpson disliked ether for several reasons:
- It could easily burst into flames.
- It bothered some patients' lungs, causing them to cough during surgery.
- It had a very strong smell.

The Growth of Public Health

COMMON CONFUSIONS

What is cholera?

Cholera is a disease that causes diarrhea (runny waste). It also causes throwing up and a high fever. Over 60 percent of people who catch it and are not treated will die. Doctors in the early 1800s had no idea what caused cholera. They did not know how it could be treated or how to stop it from spreading.

The **Industrial Revolution** began in the mid-1700s in a country called the United Kingdom, or UK. It led many people to move to cities for jobs. As the major cities grew, the places poor people lived were unsafe.

At first, the UK government did not provide clean water. It did not remove garbage or waste. As scientists now know, dirty buildings and dirty water spread **disease**. As a result, a terrible disease called **cholera** arrived (see the box at left). It killed thousands.

These crowded homes were on the Lower East Side of New York City (see pages 28 and 29).

WORD STATION
cholera deadly disease that causes diarrhea, throwing up, a high fever, and other problems

In this drawing, the clothes of cholera victims are being burned and thrown into the river in Exeter, England. Drinking water for the city came from the same river. In 1832 no one knew that cholera was passed through water.

The government jumps in

After an 1832 cholera **epidemic**, the UK government tried to fight the disease. Pressure was growing to improve clean water supplies. Cities also needed garbage collection and **sewage systems** (pipes that remove human waste).

Not again!

Cholera struck the United Kingdom again in 1848. The government finally took action. Groups called Boards of Health were set up all over the country. Local boards could take action to improve water supplies and sewage systems in their own areas.

John Snow figures it out

Cholera struck London, England, again in 1854. Most people still did not understand how it spread. Many thought it was spread in the air.

London doctor John Snow suggested that cholera entered the body through the mouth. In 1854 Snow marked every case of cholera on a map. This showed him that the **disease** had started at a public water pump. When he ordered the pump handle removed, the number of cases of cholera fell. This proved that cholera *was* spread through the water and into victims' mouths.

EDWIN CHADWICK
(1800–1890)

Edwin Chadwick collected information about the living conditions of the poor in cities throughout the United Kingdom. His report shocked the country. Chadwick was convinced that if cities were cleaner, then the people who lived there would be healthier. He helped people understand the importance of clean living conditions.

It took many years to build a sewer system for London.

Cleaning the water

By the summer of 1858, London's Thames River was full of human and animal waste. Diseases that began in the water, such as cholera, were common.

Thanks to the work of John Snow, many people now realized that dirty water caused disease. The smell of the river had also become horrible. So the government finally began work on a large **sewer system**.

New York City

The **Industrial Revolution** spread to other parts of the world. As a result, other countries were also affected by dirty and crowded cities. In the United States, the number of people in New York City grew. Many **immigrants** (people from different countries) arrived. As more people moved to New York, the city's health problems grew.

Epidemics of a **disease** called **yellow fever** struck the city in 1795, 1799, and 1803. Many people died. In 1805 a group called the Board of Health was set up. But the board did not solve many problems. Epidemics of diseases like **cholera** continued to hit. By 1850, the average New Yorker only lived to be 20 years, 8 months old!

This cartoon from the time makes fun of the first New York Board of Health. It was slow to take action.

OUR NEW YORK BOARD OF HEALTH.

WORD STATION
immigrant person who moves to and lives in a new country

Many people who lived in crowded cities, like these children, lived in terrible conditions.

HERMANN BIGGS
(1859–1923)

In New York City, Hermann Biggs was in charge of the first group in the world set up to **diagnose** diseases. He supported **vaccination** and other actions to prevent epidemics.

Improving conditions

In the mid-1800s, many people pushed for leaders to deal with the health problems in New York City. By the late 1800s, the government took a more organized approach to prevent and control diseases. For example, there were new rules about needing to inspect food and drink to make sure they were safe.

War and Changes in Medicine

During the 1800s, wars also brought about changes in **medicine**.

The Crimean War and Florence Nightingale

The Crimean War (1853–1856) was fought between the country of Russia on one side and the countries of the United Kingdom and France on the other. The war is often remembered for the story of a British nurse named Florence Nightingale.

On the battlefields of the mid–1800s, **surgeons** had to **amputate** (cut off) damaged arms and legs with saws like these.

When Nightingale first treated wounded soldiers, she found that the conditions in battlefield hospitals were dirty and crowded. By 1856 Nightingale put in place new rules and ideas. **Hygiene** (keeping things clean) was greatly improved. Hospitals were less crowded. As a result, the death rate fell from 42 percent to only 2 percent.

After she returned to the United Kingdom, Nightingale continued to make a difference. She helped set up training classes for nurses. She wrote a book that was used to train nurses. She also spoke of the importance of hygiene and clean living conditions, to prevent **disease**.

COMMON CONFUSIONS

Dangerous hospitals?

In 1857 Nightingale studied deaths in the battlefield hospitals of the Crimean War. She realized many deaths during 1854–1855 had been caused by hospital conditions, not by battlefield wounds. It was lack of water, lack of proper waste removal, and lack of fresh air that spread disease and **infections.**

Nightingale became famous as the "lady with the lamp." She would often wander through battlefield hospitals at night, to make sure the patients were being taken care of.

The Civil War

In the United States, the Civil War (1861–1865) was fought largely between northern and southern states. Southern states were trying to separate from the northern states.

A man named Jonathan Letterman was in charge of all **medical** issues for the Union Army (the army of the northern states). He introduced ideas that are still used today:

• **Ambulances** were used on the battlefield. These were vehicles that could travel to wounded soldiers. There were trained teams on each vehicle.

During the Civil War, organized transportation for the wounded was provided.

WORD STATION
ambulance vehicle that can travel quickly to people in need of medical help

- There were three different treatment stations. First, treatment areas were set up on the battlefield. Second, small battlefield hospitals were set up near the fighting, for quick treatments. Third, large hospitals were set up away from the fighting, for long-term treatment.

- The idea of **triage** was created. In triage, the wounded are put in different groups, according to how badly they need help.

The Franco-Prussian War

The Franco-Prussian War (1870–1871) was a short war between France and the German states. France eventually lost. But the countries remained very competitive with each other.

At this time, each country had a famous scientist. Louis Pasteur was in France. Robert Koch was in Germany. Each new discovery made by one of these men added to his country's pride. So they each received a lot of money to do research. Their discoveries helped move **medicine** forward.

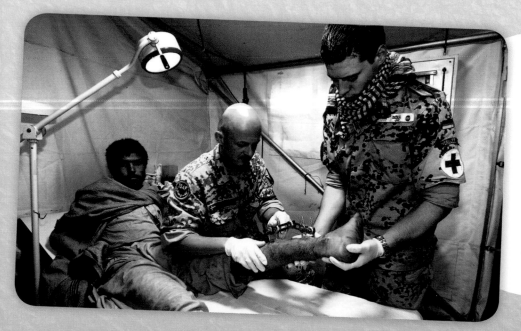

In modern wars, such as in Afghanistan, doctors and nurses still work in difficult conditions.

Women and Medicine

By the mid-1800s, many jobs were still not open to women. But things were beginning to change in the world of **medicine**.

Making nursing a respected job

When Florence Nightingale told her parents that she wanted to be a nurse, they were upset. Nurses were not respected at the time. But Nightingale changed this. In 1856 she set up her first nursing training school in London, England. Soon other schools of nursing sprung up around the world. Nursing soon became a respected job for women.

Florence Nightingale is seated at the center. Thanks to her, nursing became a respected job for women.

LINDA RICHARDS
(1841–1930)

Linda Richards was the first U.S. woman to professionally train as a nurse. She joined the first group of women to attend nurse training at the New England Hospital for Women and Children. After graduating in 1873, she worked for a year. She then spent the rest of her working life setting up colleges that trained nurses across the United States.

Women dentists

Women also became dentists in the 1800s. At first, some women learned on the job. They were not allowed to actually attend classes in colleges, though. Then, in 1865, a woman named Lucy Hobbs Taylor entered the Ohio College of Dental **Surgery**. Over time, more and more women began to train as dentists.

At last, Dr. Blackwell

When women first tried to become doctors, their biggest problem was getting accepted into **medical** school. Few women attended college at the time.

When 26-year-old Elizabeth Blackwell decided to train as a doctor, she was turned down by 29 medical schools. Finally, she was accepted by the Geneva Medical School in New York. She graduated at the top of her class in 1849. In 1857 she set up a New York hospital for women and children. She worked in hospitals and as a teacher for the rest of her life.

When Elizabeth Blackwell started medical school, some male students refused to attend classes.

By setting up medical schools and hospitals, Elizabeth Garrett Anderson made sure women could get training as doctors and nurses.

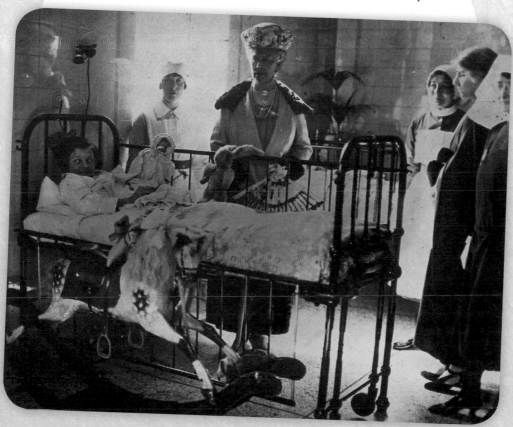

GEORGIA ARBUCKLE FIX
(1852–1928)

Georgia Arbuckle Fix was the first woman to attend the Omaha Medical College, in Nebraska. She graduated in 1883. Three years later, she moved near the border of what is now the state of Wyoming. Few people lived there at the time. For many years, Fix was the only doctor within 75 miles (120 kilometers).

From nurse to doctor

British nurse Elizabeth Garrett Anderson wanted to follow Blackwell's example. For four years, she applied to every college and hospital in England to study **medicine**. They all turned her down. In 1865 she found a group that would allow her to take the tests needed to become a doctor. Anderson became a successful doctor. She set up several teaching hospitals that trained women.

The Brain and the Mind

At the beginning of the **Industrial Revolution**, people did not know much about how the brain worked. By the end of the 1800s, this changed greatly.

Mapping the brain

During the 1800s, scientists greatly improved their understanding of the brain. Scientists performed experiments on animals. They observed patients with damage to specific parts of the brain (see the box on page 39). This showed that different parts of the brain were involved in different functions, such as the ability to speak.

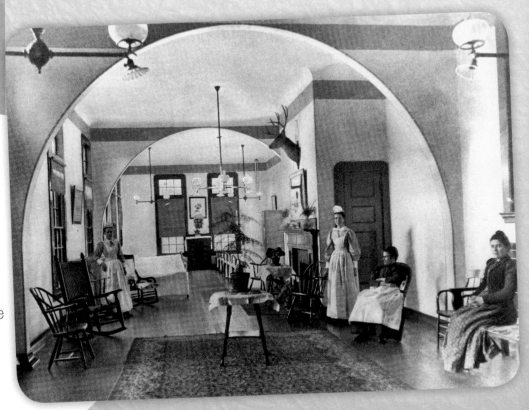

This picture was taken in 1900, at the Boston Insane Hospital. By this time, people with mental problems received better care than they had in the past.

WORD STATION
mental relating to the mind

Sigmund Freud studied patients' dreams. He felt that dreams show people's true desires. Doctors built upon his ideas in the 1900s.

Phineas Gage was a U.S. railroad construction worker. He was hurt in an 1848 explosion. The blast forced a long metal bar through one side of his skull and out the other. Gage survived. But after the accident, his personality completely changed. He became violent. He swore all the time. Gage's injuries and the effects they had on him helped doctors pinpoint a part of the brain. This part controls personality and social **inhibitions** (the ability to control rude behavior).

It's all in the mind

By the late 1800s, German doctors such as Wilhelm Wundt and Emil Kraepelin started to research a wide variety of **mental** illnesses. These are illnesses of the mind.

Meanwhile, people like Sigmund Freud developed a treatment for mental problems known as **psychoanalysis**. This involved studying both normal thoughts and **unconscious** thoughts. These are thoughts that people do not know they are thinking.

The Medical Revolution

The years from the beginning of the **Industrial Revolution** to the beginning of the 1900s are often called the "**medical revolution**." A revolution is huge change in how something works. **Medicine** was able to make huge steps forward thanks to several developments.

Understanding germs and disease

The most important thing that happened during this period was understanding how **germs** and **disease** were spread. Once this was understood, it was possible to try to prevent the spread of diseases. It was also possible to develop treatments.

MEDICINE AROUND THE WORLD

By 1900 good medical treatment was common in the wealthiest countries of the world, such as the United States and the United Kingdom. But poorer countries did not usually experience these kinds of treatments.

Clara Barton and the Red Cross

After the Civil War, U.S. nurse Clara Barton (see page 32) traveled to Europe. She was very impressed by the work of a group there called the Red Cross. In 1881 Barton and others founded the American Red Cross Society in the United States. The new group worked to help and treat people hurt in war. Over time, it also worked to help people affected by natural disasters such as floods. Thanks to the work of the Red Cross, millions of people affected by war and disaster have been helped since 1881.

WORD STATION
revolution huge change in how something works

In the 1800s, a tool called the stethoscope was introduced. It allows doctors to listen to patients' hearts and other sounds in the body. The stethoscope shown here is an early form of the tool. **Technology** like this changed medicine forever.

Improvements

The new **antiseptics** gave doctors and nurses an important tool to stop **infection** from spreading. It also made **surgery** safer. **Anesthetics** managed patients' pain. Hospitals and cities became cleaner and safer. And doctors and nurses began to get solid training.

But the greatest gift to the medical revolution came from the ideas and discoveries of talented people. Their ideas and hard work helped make life better for everyone.

Timeline

mid-1700s	The **Industrial Revolution** begins. This leads to new **technology**. It also leads to people crowding into cities for work. This leads to health problems.
mid-1700s	The technology of the **microscope** is improved
1765	The first North American **medical** school is formed. It is the Philadelphia Medical College, in the state of Pennsylvania.
1796	English doctor Edward Jenner introduces his **vaccination** against **smallpox**
1832	The first great **cholera epidemics** occur in the United Kingdom and the United States
1844	Ignaz Semmelweis notices that doctors are spreading **disease** in a hospital in Austria
1845	U.S. dentist Horace Wells first uses **ether**
1846	**Anesthetics** are first used in **surgery**
1847	**Chloroform** is used in childbirth
1847	The American **Medical** Association is formed
1849	Elizabeth Blackwell graduates at the top of her medical school class
1853–1856	The Crimean War is fought. Florence Nightingale works to improve nursing and military conditions.
1854	John Snow figures out that water is responsible for the spread of cholera

1861–1865	The Civil War is fought. Clara Barton becomes known for her brave work to help soldiers wounded in battle.
1862	Louis Pasteur writes about how **germs** work
mid-1860s	Joseph Lister realizes that germs cause **infections**
1865	Lister uses **carbolic acid** as an **antiseptic** in surgery
1866	The government of New York sets up a special group to keep track of health issues in New York City
1870s	Robert Koch identifies the germs that cause different diseases
1895	Sigmund Freud reveals his first work on **psychoanalysis**
c. 1900	The Industrial Revolution starts to come to an end

Glossary

ambulance vehicle that can travel quickly to people in need of medical help

amputate cut off

anesthetic substance used during surgery to stop a patient from feeling pain

antiseptic substance that kills tiny, harmful living things

autopsy examination of a body to find out the cause of death

carbolic acid powerful substance that can kill harmful microorganisms

chloroform substance that was once used to relieve pain

cholera deadly disease that causes diarrhea, throwing up, a high fever, and other problems

contaminate make unclean by contact with something dirty or infected

court place where people accused of crimes appear before a judge and possibly receive a punishment, such as time in jail

diagnose identify a disease or injury by studying it closely

disease health problem that prevents the body from working correctly

dissect cut up a dead body in order to study it

epidemic fast spread of a disease through an area or group of people

ether strong substance that was breathed in to relieve pain

factory large building with machines used to make things

germ microorganism that causes disease

hygiene practice of maintaining health by keeping clean

immigrant person who moves to and lives in a new country

Industrial Revolution period from the mid-1700s through the 1800s when machines and factories changed daily life and many people moved to cities

infection when tiny living things enter the body and make a person sick

inhibition ability to control certain behaviors that could be considered rude

inoculation another word for vaccination

medical relating to medicine

medicine science of treating and preventing illness

mental relating to the mind

microorganism very tiny living thing

microscope tool used to see very small objects

midwife specially trained nurse who helps women with childbirth

pasteurization process that involves heating a liquid for set lengths of time to destroy germs

psychoanalysis treatment for mental problems, focusing on the conscious mind (what people know they are thinking) and the unconscious mind (what people do not know they are thinking)

pus thick, yellowish substance in infected sores

revolution huge change in how something works

sewage system system of pipes that removes human waste from areas where people live

smallpox disease that causes blisters on the face and often leads to death

sterilize make free of harmful microorganisms (tiny living things)

surgeon person who performs surgery

surgery treatment of disease or injuries with an operation rather than drugs

technology machine or tool resulting from science

triage system in which wounded people are put in different groups, according to their different treatment needs

unconscious describes thoughts people do not know they are having

vaccination introducing a substance (called a vaccine) into the body so the person does not catch a disease

yellow fever disease that causes a high fever and can be deadly

Find Out More

Books

Ballard, Carol. *From Cowpox to Antibiotics: Discovering Vaccines and Medicine* (Chain Reactions). Chicago: Heinemann Library, 2006.

Clare, John D. *Medicine in the Industrial World* (History of Medicine). New York: Enchanted Lion, 2006.

Hartman, Eve, and Wendy Meshbesher. *The Scientists Behind Medical Advances* (Sci-Hi Scientists). Chicago: Raintree, 2011.

Vickers, Rebecca. *Medicine* (From Fail to Win!). Chicago: Raintree, 2011.

Websites

www.johnsnowsociety.org/johnsnow/facts.html
This website will give you a lot of information about Dr. John Snow and his work to trace the source of cholera epidemics.

www.knowitall.org/kidswork/hospital/ history/17_19century/index.html
This history of medicine written for kids includes facts about the 1800s.

nmhm.washingtondc.museum/exhibits/nationswounds
This website of the National Museum of Health and Medicine explores medicine during the Civil War. Learn more facts about medicine during this war and see lots of interesting photos.

www.tenement.org
This is the website of the Lower East Side Tenement Museum. It gives you virtual tours and lots of information about life in the poor areas of New York City in the 1800s.

Places to visit

The Exploratorium, San Francisco, California
www.exploratorium.edu

The Health Museum, Houston, Texas
www.mhms.org

International Museum of Surgical Science, Chicago, Illinois
www.imss.org

National Museum of Civil War Medicine, Frederick, Maryland
www.civilwarmed.org

National Museum of Health and Medicine, Washington, D.C.
nmhm.washingtondc.museum

The Tenement Museum, New York City
www.tenement.org

More topics to research

Learn more about discoveries, advances in technology, and events:

- How were microscopes improved?

- How were sewage systems and water supplies improved?

- What changes happened in medical and nursing schools?

- What opportunities were available for women in medicine?

- How were governments involved in improving people's health, especially the health of people living in large cities?

- The cover of this book shows a detail from a painting of Florence Nightingale helping a patient in Turkey. Find out more about how Nightingale changed the study and practice of nursing after she returned to England.

Index